An Indescribable Beauty

AN INDESCRIBABLE BEAUTY

Letters home to Germany from Wellington, New Zealand
1859 & 1862

———◆———

Friedrich August Krull

AWA PRESS

First edition published in 2012 by
Awa Press, Level One, 85 Victoria Street, Wellington, New Zealand.

Introduction and Epilogue © Oliver Harrison 2012
Edited text of letters © Awa Press 2012

The letters in this volume were originally written in German.
The translator of this English version is unknown.

National Library of New Zealand Cataloguing-in-Publication Data
Krull, Friedrich, 1836–1914. An indescribable beauty : letters home to Germany from Wellington, New Zealand, 1859 & 1862 / author: Friedrich Krull ; historical editor: Mary Varnham ; introduction and epilogue by Oliver Harrison.
ISBN 978-1-877551-33-8
1. Krull, Friedrich, 1836-1914—Correspondence.
2. Germans—New Zealand—Wellington—Correspondence.
3. Maori (New Zealand people)—New Zealand—Wellington (Region)—History—19th century.
4. Wellington (N.Z. : Region)—History—19th century.
5. Wellington (N.Z. : Region)—Description and travel. [1. Kōrero nehe. reo 2. Noho-ā-iwi. reo]
I. Varnham, Mary. II. Title.
993.602—dc 22

This book is typeset in Black Knight FLF and Mrs Eaves XL.
Design and typesetting by Greg Simpson, Wellington.
Front cover illustration by Charles Emilius Gold, A-288-029, Alexander Turnbull Library.
Printed by Everbest Printing Company, China.

www.awapress.com

Published with the support of

ARTS COUNCIL OF NEW ZEALAND TOI AOTEAROA

'We have a high opinion of German emigrants;
they are sober, industrious and Christian men,
and we gladly hail their introduction among our own
countrymen as likely to lead to the happiest results.
... We belong to a common race; we are, despite our English
pride of nationality, governed by German monarchs;
so that the fellow-feeling between Germans and Englishmen
is easily accounted for.'

————•————

New Zealand Journal, June 1844

CONTENTS

———•———

Wellington Harbour, looking towards
Matiu/Somes Island and the eastern hills, 1880s.

WATERCOLOUR BY JANE STOWE

Publisher's note

———•———

Ａt the ninetieth birthday celebration of my cousin Jim Krull a relation handed me a crumpled and yellowing typescript. 'You may find this interesting,' he said.

Jim is related to me paternally: his mother, Dorothy, was my father's sister. A sweet, un-self-regarding woman, Dorothy had married Fritz Krull, a man more than twenty years her senior. Fritz was a legend in our family. Not only had he fought in the Boer War, he was also German. When I knew him he was as old as Methuselah, a wiry stick of a man with spiky white hair, a ferocious temper, a love of anchovies, and a passion for playing the game of draughts, which he had to win or be damned. When he occasionally came to stay with us—mostly to give poor Aunt Dorothy some respite—he and my father would argue endlessly. 'Fritz is an old fool,' Dad would sigh the moment his brother-in-law left to return to his home in Feilding. Beyond this I knew nothing of his background.

Some time after the party I came across the scruffy little document. It turned out to be the English translation of a series of letters that Fritz's father, Friedrich Krull, had written home to his mother in Germany after his arrival in New Zealand in

1859. In an idle moment I began to read the fading script. I was not sanguine: as a publisher I read many submissions and most have the interest and excitement of a vacuum-cleaner manual. But within minutes, to my surprise, I was completely absorbed, transported back 152 years to a world and a city and a country I thought I knew intimately, but in fact had experienced not at all.

The dry facts of history are always fascinating. I was aware that Wellington, my home town, had been settled first by Māori, who made villages and pa around the beautiful, bountiful, wind-ravaged coastline. I understood that the original iwi had in due course been ousted by others from the north, and that today two of these invading tribes, Te Ātiawa and Ngāti Toa, still contest much of the territory and mana of the place. I knew that whalers and sealers had plundered Cook Strait and that white settlers, most from depressed parts of Britain, had arrived from 1840 onwards, duped Māori out of their land, filled in large tracts of the harbour, built a town of wood, masonry and brick, burnt off the bush, thrown sheep on to every patch of cleared earth, and generally brought what was fondly known as 'civilisation' to the natives.

But reading these letters written by Friedrich Krull was like seeing a 3-D movie for the first time. Here was a young man, fresh off the boat, starting a new life among strangers on the other side of the known world. And not only was the twenty-two year old adventurous, setting out within days to explore the countryside on horseback, he also had a consuming curiosity to meet and learn more about the country's indigenous inhabitants. And he could write. From the first lyrical sentences, Krull was such a poignant presence I felt as though I were taking the journey with him.

To read these letters is an experience tinged with sadness. The bush of indescribable beauty is now largely gone. The captivating parrots that hopped and swarmed about have long since disappeared from the mainland, as have most of the raucous songbirds. The small villages where Māori came out of whare and offered passing travellers food and drink are, where anything at all remains, the realm of archaeology. And the land grabs and wars that Krull innocently thinks have been averted in fact went on to create deep divisions, inequalities and resentments that persist today.

But there is a quiet joy here too. I was often reminded of T.S. Eliot's lines: 'We shall not cease from exploration, and the end of all our exploring will be to arrive where we started and know the place for the first time.' Wellington was never going to be the workers' paradise of which Krull and his fellow settlers dreamed. Like all cities it is flawed, clumsy, and ridden with human mistakes that keep on coming. But it is also a place of natural beauty, of quiet promise, and of a welcome to strangers.

Working on this book it was not long before I came across others who knew of the Krull letters. In particular, I was thrilled to discover a PhD thesis by Oliver Harrison entitled *The Paradise of the Southern Hemisphere: The Perception of New Zealand and the Māori in Written Accounts of German-speaking Explorers and Travellers 1839–1889*, in which a chapter is devoted to Friedrich Krull. I also learned that a version of the letters, together with their original German text, had been published in *Von Mecklenburg nach Neuseeland* (2002), a collaboration between the Neubrandenburg Regional Museum, Germany, and the University of Auckland's Research Centre for Germanic Connections with New Zealand and the Pacific.

I am indebted to Oliver Harrison for his contribution to the book, particularly his wonderful introduction and epilogue that set the Krull letters in the wider context of early German contact with New Zealand and provide interesting information on Krull's later life. It is a little known fact that, after the British, Germans were the largest immigrant group in nineteenth-century New Zealand. A great many people in New Zealand are of German descent, including of course Jim (or Eric, as he was christened), his late sister Mary, Mary's three children Caroline, Martin and Bill, and grandchildren Lucy, Harriet and James.

My thanks go, too, to Jenna Tinkle, Fiona Kirkcaldie and Kylie Sutcliffe, who have made this book come alive through their assiduous image research. This has enabled us to include interesting, sometimes startling, contemporary photographs, paintings and drawings alongside the letters, including many of people and places that Friedrich Krull visited on his travels.

Finally, I would like to thank Vincent O'Malley of History Works for his knowledgeable, meticulous and often enlightening investigation of many of the people and incidents that appear in the letters, and his fellow historians Bruce Stirling, also of HistoryWorks, and Angela Ballara for their assistance.

Mary Varnham
Wellington

Introduction

———•———

I n 2003 I embarked on a doctoral thesis about German-speaking explorers and travellers in nineteenth-century New Zealand. While New Zealand immigration schemes in the mid nineteenth century looked mainly to Britain, German immigrants were also considered valuable; in time they would become the second largest settler group. Most came from northern Germany, while others arrived from the Rhineland, Bavaria and other German-speaking areas such as Austria, Switzerland and Bohemia. For these Germans, the young colony on the other side of the globe offered the promise of a better life—a chance to gain an 'independency' and freedom from land-owning aristocracy. They were, in turn, seen as desirable: industrious, reliable and of sober habits.

The first plan was for a German colony to be established on the Chathams, a group of islands that then lay beyond the eastern boundary of New Zealand. Proposed between late 1839 and 1842 by the New Zealand Company, with the cooperation of the Hamburg-based German Colonisation Company, the idea came to nothing when the British government declared the company had no legal right to purchase land on the islands.

In 1843 and 1844 two attempts were made to attract German immigrants to the Nelson region at the top of the South Island. The first was spearheaded by John Nicholas Beit, the German agent for the New Zealand Company. It would prove disastrous. After settlers arrived on the *St Pauli* they founded the village of St Paulidorf in the Moutere Valley but the land turned out to be flood-prone and in less than a year the village was abandoned. Meanwhile, another group had arrived on board a ship named the *Skiold*, their passages financed by an aristocrat, Count Kuno zu Rantzau-Breitenburg. Rantzau and several agents had secured a large area of land on which the settlers were to be indentured labourers. The settlement of Ranzau on the fertile Waimea plain flourished and still exists today; it was renamed Hope in 1914.

In the early 1860s another wave of Germans arrived to seek their fortunes in the gold rushes of Central Otago, Marlborough and the West Coast, and in 1863 the government proposed introducing German migrants as 'military settlers' in Taranaki with the aid of a Hamburg merchant firm, J.C. Godeffroy & Son, and the respected leader Johann Friederich August (Fedor) Kelling as government agent. This failed to get off the ground.

A decade later German immigration reached its peak under Prime Minister Julius Vogel's assisted immigrants and public works scheme. Vogel's vision was to build roads and railways that would open up previously inaccessible land to agriculture and farming. To carry out the work, new settlers were sought from Germany and Scandinavia as well as Britain.

In time further German-speaking settlements and communities would be established: in Northland (Houhora, Awanui), Auckland (Pūhoi, Pukekohe), Waikato (Ōhaupō), Taranaki (Inglewood, Midhirst, Stratford, Eltham, Kaimiro, Rātāpiko,

Fedor Kelling, emigration agent, farmer and first German
elected to New Zealand parliament, circa 1895.

Tarata), Hawke's Bay (Norsewood, Napier, Takapau, Makaretu), Wellington-Rangitikei (Marton, Rongotea, Halcombe, Carterton), Nelson (Sarau, Rosental, Neudorf, Hanover, Schönbach), Westland (Jackson's Bay, Smoothwater Valley, Hokitika), Canterbury (Germantown, Waimate, Hanover Valley, Marshlands, Oxford, German Bay), Otago (Waihola, Allanton, German Hill) and Southland (Gore, Germantown).

✥ ✥ ✥

Set against this backdrop was the emergence of what are known today as the New Zealand Wars. At first it was not much of a concern to European settlers if Māori tribes fought among themselves. However, it was another matter when fighting affected the colonists' own well-being and interests. The first portent of interracial conflict came on June 17, 1843 with a fatal confrontation at Wairau between armed Nelson settlers and local Māori led by Te Rauparaha and Te Rangihaeata of Ngāti Toa, over land to which the Europeans had incorrectly assumed rights.

Major conflicts followed: the Northern War (1845–46) in the Bay of Islands, led by Ngāpuhi chiefs Hone Heke and Kawiti; the Taranaki War (1860–61), involving both the southern Taranaki tribes and the King movement, which spread beyond its borders into neighbouring tribal regions right through the North Island; the Waikato War (1863–64), which saw troops invade King country in the Waikato in an attempt to break the backbone of 'Māori independence'. From 1868 to 1872 there was further conflict in Tauranga, and skirmishes with Riwha Titokowaru in south Taranaki and Whanganui, and with Te Kooti Arikirangi Te

Tūruki in the Bay of Plenty, Poverty Bay, Taupō, East Cape and northern Hawke's Bay.

Such conflict was bound to influence views of Māori and the suitability of the colony for immigration, yet in popular German publications of the day writers tended to side with Māori and stress their barbaric treatment at the hands of the British. For many, a 'Vernichtungskrieg'—war of extermination—was being waged against the brave and courageous Māori people, which would lead to their eventual demise and replacement by the increasing number of Europeans pouring into the country.

This sympathetic viewpoint was shared by many German-speaking visitors to the colony. Furthermore, their not being British could prove an advantage in winning the trust of Māori, allowing them to meet high-ranking Māori leaders and gain permission to visit closely guarded or sacred sites. This gave their written accounts inherent value: their observations and perspectives did not simply reinforce the British status quo.

During my research I came across the letters of Friedrich Krull, a young man in his early twenties who arrived in New Zealand in 1859 and soon became the country's first German Consul. Born in 1836 in the Grand Duchy of Mecklenburg Strelitz in Neubrandenburg, Krull had attended Gotha's Commercial College in 1853, following in the footsteps of his merchant father, Georg Friedrich Krull. Seeing no future for himself in Germany, he had then spent several years working in a merchant's office in France before travelling to London and embarking with his friend Karl Hartmann on a Swedish ship, the *Equator*, bound

The *Equator*, on which Friedrich Krull sailed from England
to New Zealand, a voyage of four months.

PENCIL AND CHINESE WHITE DRAWING BY WILLIAM REES

for the young and promising land of New Zealand. The ship set sail on September 18, 1858 and the two young men reached Wellington, their new home, on January 22, 1859.

Before departing, Krull had been asked by his brother-in-law Ernst Boll, a well-known Neubrandenburg historian, natural scientist and secretary of the Friends of Mecklenburg Natural History, to send reports of life in the new colony. Together with descriptions of Wellington life, Krull would soon recount three excursions he made with Hartmann into the Māori-populated regions of Wellington province. On February 4 the two men travelled on horseback with two guides through the Hutt Valley, Rimutakas and Wairarapa; on February 14 they visited a Māori pa, probably Kaiwherowhero, in South Wairarapa, and on April 4 they departed on a considerable journey through Porirua, Horokiwi Valley, Paekākāriki, Waikanae and Ōtaki. Three years later, on January 26, 1862, Krull would also visit the German settlement of Ranzau near Nelson.

The letters of these journeys, which he addressed to his mother, form the heart of this book. They are sensitive and in many ways extraordinary. Krull not only meets and describes some notable Māori leaders of the time, but also turns a keen eye on both the landscape and the people who occupy it.

To read these letters is to experience a New Zealand that can now only be imagined. Much of the countryside is resplendent in beautiful bush, there are so many birds that at times conversation is difficult, Māori farm large tracts of land and live in peaceful villages, and life for European settlers is good, if somewhat expensive. The region in which he lives and travels, the lower North Island, is as yet unaffected by racial conflict, although storm clouds are gathering.

Sadly, the correspondence published by Boll in the appendix of *Archiv des Vereins der Freunde der Naturgeschichte in Mecklenburg* in 1859 and 1862 are the only existing letters from Krull's early travels in New Zealand. A revised and updated version of his early travels also appeared anonymously in *Das Ausland* as 'Mittheilungen aus Neuseeland' in a more condensed and generalised form in January 1860. This journal had a wider circulation, and the material had been edited to conform to a more popular, informative and reader-friendly format. The translated text in this book comes from the original letters, which are the more detailed and impressionistic.

Friedrich Krull wrote with a particular audience in mind: the prospective immigrant. As emigration became a feasible and affordable solution to tough socio-economic conditions, many Germans were interested in information that outlined the pros and cons of living and working in foreign colonies. As a new immigrant himself, and one with a merchant background, Krull was in a good position to provide such advice.

On his arrival he captures the ambience of a fledgling British colony well on its way towards becoming a 'worker's paradise' through hard work and perseverance. Later, as German Consul, he witnesses fellow Mecklenburgers leading by example through their industrious ways in New Zealand's healthy and paradisiacal, albeit temperamental, climate. The actions of both settlers and government are viewed according to the best interests of the colony and its future prosperity but there's a twist: while he sees that land needs to be provided for immigrants, he does not believe this should be at the expense of Māori and views their loss of land with sadness. He considers Māori an intelligent, friendly and self-sufficient people who are on the whole better educated than his fellow Germans and live more civilised and prosperous lives, particularly around the hot lakes district. At the same time he provides original insights into their peaceable and productive yet subjugated and materialistic state. His letters are therefore a unique contribution to the depiction of colonial life in New Zealand.

Oliver Harrison
Sydney

January 27th
1859

Mount Egmont/Taranaki and Sugar Loaf/Ngā Motu Islands, 1849.

WATERCOLOUR AND CHINESE WHITE DRAWING BY CHARLES HEAPHY

With a favourable wind we were now approaching our new home. On the morning of January 15th we saw land, the snow-capped Mount Egmont, and towards sunset this mountain and a large part of the country appeared in their whole glory.

The next morning we had no wind and remained anchored only five miles from land. It was a lovely day, the first really warm and perfect one since we had left the Cape.[1] From the distance we could observe the beautiful coast before us. The mountain rose in many terraces to its summit and offered under its hood of gleaming snow a wonderful sight. Two small green parrots—the only species of their kind—flew on board but we tried in vain to catch them.

On the 17th the wind rose again, but not in our favour as we drifted towards the South Island. On the following two days we advanced only very slowly and our impatience to reach Wellington increased more and more. We had only to sail around a projecting bluff and we would have been there, but against a westerly gale this was impossible to accomplish. At four in the afternoon we got into a thick fog, and as we were

Wellington Harbour and sailing craft, circa 1850s.

near land on a very rocky coast our position became dangerous and we had to make for the sea again.

The next morning at seven o'clock the fog dispersed and a favourable wind helped us sail around the aforementioned bluff. We were now only a few miles from the harbour entrance called Port Nicholson. The pilot was already on board when again the wind changed and forced us to anchor. So near our destination and still unable to reach it!

On the 20th we were still becalmed but we now had a chance to get a view of our future home, which was lying before us in the superb beauty of its green wilderness. Everywhere we saw huge smoke clouds rising: to be able to cultivate the land the farmers were burning down the bush. The fires had a wonderful effect when it became dark.

The pilot had brought some flowers with him and we greeted these products of our new home with great joy. Although they were all well-known European flowers—fuchsias, pelargoniums, roses and irises—I cannot remember ever having seen such magnificent colouring, but perhaps my eyes were deceived as it was such a long time since I had seen any flowers.

It was the 22nd of January when at last the wind was in our favour. With great alacrity we helped the sailors weigh anchor, and with what suspense did H[2] and I stand on the foredeck to get our first view of the town that was to become our new home. After we entered through the narrow straits a beautiful harbour lay before us, surrounded by high hills, and behind it more hills ascending to the snowline. Right in the east we saw Wellington itself, stretching along the coast for a mile. We were amazed: we had not expected the place to be so big.

We anchored at three o'clock and a few minutes later we

entered the town, which was full of life as the nineteenth anniversary of its foundation was being celebrated. It was in 1840 that the first settlement was established and now there are more than 7,000 Europeans living here.[3] Flags hung from the houses, guns were booming from the citadel, and races and regattas were in full swing.

The houses are all built of wood and one-storeyed, which gives the town the appearance of a village. They are built very simply on account of the frequent earthquakes. That's why neither here nor in other places do you find houses built of stone. There are generally only four rooms in a house, including the kitchen, and also a verandah and small garden in front.

The natives, who call themselves Māori, number in Wellington about 200.[4] Of their customs I shall tell you more by and by: at present I know too little about them. The men are of fine appearance. They are all wonderfully tattooed, but not the children so in time to come their facial decoration will disappear. Many natives are clad in European clothes, but the greater part wear, as an only garment, a red or white blanket. At present there is a big meeting of the tribes in the interior for the purpose of electing a king.

In the evening, when the festivities were over, we went to a hotel which, although supposed to be the best one here, is only very average. Our bed, breakfast, dinner and evening meal cost each of us 15/– which surprised us very much, but before long we had still more opportunities to be surprised at the prices here. On Sunday morning (the 23rd) we went to the English church. We had to spend the rest of the day at our hotel because of constant rain, but we enjoyed ourselves in the company of some very jovial gentlemen who had come by steamer from Auckland.

Te Aro flat in Wellington around the time of Friedrich Krull's arrival.

Typical Thorndon cottage, Molesworth Street, 1860s.

They had travelled far and wide and talked about India and the Dutch colonies, but everybody declared that New Zealand was the better land.

On Monday we set about trying to rent a small house, thinking this would help us to get a more home-like feeling. We inspected a small, miserable cottage with three rooms and a kitchen in a distant part of the town. The walls were neither papered nor painted and yet the rent was £1 per week. They wanted still more money for a second dwelling we looked at. We then thought of buying, but the prices of £600 and £800 scared us too much.

Everything is very expensive here. There is a great lack of workmen and consequently their demands for wages are very high. However, trade is extensive. There are representatives of large firms who have fleeced the place for years and, through the power of their money, monopolised business. In this respect Wellington disappointed us: we did not expect to find such strong competition and did not think that living here would be as expensive as it is. We have now decided to live in a boarding house until we find a suitable cottage. We pay £1/10– weekly for room and food. All our baggage is at the Custom House and for that reason we have delayed the announcement of our establishment.

The development of this colony is rapidly going forward with a brilliant future in sight. Nature's beauties, especially the vegetation, have fulfilled nearly all our expectations, but Wellington is supposed to be the least favoured place concerning the weather.

February 25th

1859

Twenty-eight-year-old German geologist
Ferdinand von Hochstetter, 1859.

LITHOGRAPH BY ADOLF DAUTHAGE

We are still in our boarding house, where we find it very pleasant, especially as there is no lack of interesting people. Two of the boarders have been in nearly all the British colonies. They have been travelling for the last ten years for their own pleasure and are highly cultured men, very keen on research work for they have a whole laboratory with them. They are in contact with Dr Hochstetter[5] in Auckland at present and have exchanged many specimens with him. As we have time before we start in business we intend to take a trip into the interior, where the natives, in whom I am especially interested, are still living in accordance with their old customs and rules.

The above plan was carried out on February 4th. We hired five horses and two Māori, young strong fellows who under-stood English sufficiently to be able to talk to us. The fifth horse served as a packhorse. We took with us some clothes, my woollen blanket, some bottles of wine and gin, tobacco, cigars, clay pipes and small toys.

The sun had hardly risen on the 4th when our horses with their wild riders were at our door. We slung our rifles across our shoulders, fastened our loaded revolvers on our saddles, and off we went at full gallop. Our guides were really fine-looking with their beautifully tattooed faces, and wore no other garment than a dirty white blanket hung around their necks, which gave them some likeness to the Bedouins.

We followed the road leading to the Wairarapa valley and soon arrived at Hutt,[6] a small town of about 2,000 inhabitants right across from Wellington at the opposite side of the harbour. A river streams through the valley and turns it into one of the most beautiful and richest districts in Wellington province. Nearly all the land is cultivated—the bush burnt and the ground partially cleared of the roots—but as this work is very costly because of the high wages you see many dead trunks, which give the place, especially in moonlight, a wild and weird appearance.

The forest, called 'bush', is of an indescribable beauty. It consists of magnificent very tall trees covered with glistening green foliage, the leaves of which don't resemble those of our trees in the least. A luxurious creeper climbs into the highest branches and thousands of carmine-coloured blossoms glisten between the green leaves. The growth is so strong that you have to use an axe to get through the thicket.

Between and below these high trees grow the ferns, the shining pearls of the forest. I have never seen anything like this. A common kind resembles a palm.[7] The long branchless stem is 40 to 50 feet high, and often it is entwined by a creeper whose blossoms resemble our myrtles. This tree is very useful to the farmers: it serves for making fences and building whare.

View across Hutt Valley to Wellington Harbour with Percy's Flour Mill
in the foreground, late 1860s.

PHOTOGRAPH BY JAMES BRAGGE

Dense bush and still water,
possibly Hutt Forest and River, circa 1850.

WATERCOLOUR BY CHARLES EMILIUS GOLD

Kākāriki, New Zealand parakeets, 1839. The three species—red-crowned, yellow-crowned and orange-fronted—were once plentiful.

WATERCOLOUR BY CHARLES HEAPHY

This wonderful forest scene is enhanced by thousands of birds. A small green parrot with a long tail, a red topknot and blue feathers in its wings is the commonest bird here.[8] There were thousands of them hopping about and swarming round us, but we also heard many singing birds with prettily coloured plumage.

We passed many lonely farms and native settlements, but did not stop to inspect their whare as they are too European already—we wanted to wait until we came to the more isolated, uncivilised places. Our guides told us the history of each tribe as we passed through their land: what wars had taken place, how under this or that tree they had slaughtered their prisoners, and the bloodthirsty vengeance of the enemy chiefs. When we passed through their villages the people ran out of their whare and greeted us most cordially, offering us food and drink. Our rifles and revolvers caught their eyes at once and they offered to pay £20 for a revolver, but as there is a high penalty for selling arms to natives we, of course, did not commit ourselves.[9]

After riding forty miles I was so tired I could not go any further and at three o'clock in the afternoon we decided to make a halt and spend the night in the open. We chose a lovely place; we cleared a space under a tree with our axes and made a camp while our horses grazed some distance away.

While H and I got a fire going our men went away, hoping to get a bird for our supper. We had to wait a long time for their return and were beginning to fear they had vanished with horses and guns, when suddenly a shot rang out and the joyous exclamation 'Kapai!' Some minutes later our wild friends returned with beaming faces and a turkey. There are many turkeys and wild fowls about, but as they are very shy it is not easy to shoot them. The plucking and cleaning took only fifteen minutes, then a long stick was put right through the animal. The guides, after continually turning it over the fire for about half an hour, declared that the roasting was sufficiently done, and it certainly tasted so good that we devoured it until only the bones were left.

Two Māori men and a seated woman
with tree fern at sunset, possibly Hutt Valley, circa 1848.

WATERCOLOUR AND GOUACHE ON PAPER
BY FREDERICK JOHN WHITE

All through the night we kept the fire going and at daybreak we decamped and continued our journey. We were now leaving the road through the Hutt Valley and had to undertake the crossing of the high Rimutakas to get into the Wairarapa district. This was a difficult task for our horses, and as I was not used to riding I got very tired.

After having made twenty to twenty-six miles we stopped at the station of a Scottish farmer named M.[10] Here we got a very kind reception. He showed us his herds, which consisted of about 2,000 head of cattle. Further away he had 5,000 sheep. He is very rich as he bought his land straight from the Māori, which is now the prerogative only of the English government. He bought 200,000 acres at one penny per acre, while the government now sells the land for 10/– per acre.[11]

The following morning we did not leave the station until eleven o'clock, and although we would have been able to reach the Ruamahanga River, the home of our guides, we decided to stay the night at an inn. The accommodation was miserable, and next morning we made our entry into the pa.[12] We were conducted to the chief Te Turuatakiti. I estimated his age at about thirty-eight to forty years. He wore European clothes but his face was tattooed all over. His facial expression was mild but firm. In his ear he wore a shark's tooth; his body was slim but strong; his hair was curly. His wife, who came to meet us with a smoking pipe between her lips, was also tattooed, but not as much as her husband. The only garment she wore was a dirty shirt. Both greeted us in their national fashion by rubbing noses with us. While this is going on they make a noise like a bumblebee, or mutter and groan. The longer the performance lasts, and the louder it gets, the more friendly it is supposed to be.

Māori family at a cutting alongside the Rimutaka hill road, 1854.

WATERCOLOUR AND INK DRAWING BY JOHN PEARSE

Māori family outside a wharepuni, small communal sleeping house,
at Mangakuta near Masterton, 1870s.

PHOTOGRAPHER UNKNOWN

We went through this ceremony with every member of the family and were then conducted into the house, which was nothing but a one-room hut made of logs and roofed in with bark and leaves. The centre was occupied by a fireplace. They all live and sleep here.

We presented the chief with a bottle of brandy, his wife with two clay pipes and some cigars, and there were toys for the children. Our arms were again the object of general admiration and the chief offered us all sorts of goods for them. He understood very little English and could not speak it at all, so our guides had to act as interpreters.

At about ten a.m., after we had rested for a little while on the bare ground as there was nothing resembling a chair or seat, a meal consisting of bread, ham, fish and potatoes was served. It looked disgusting and we lost all appetite, but a fierce look from the chief, a sign of his anger, forced us to partake. We were provided with knives and forks, and also plates made of New Zealand flax.

The cooking is done in this way: stones are made red-hot in the fire, then a hole a foot deep is dug into the ground. This is lined with the stones, and green leaves are placed on them. The fish, meat and potatoes follow, covered with more green leaves, then earth is thrown over everything so no steam can escape. A fire is lit on top and after about half an hour this is carefully cleared away, as is all the earth. The food is lifted out with two sticks and placed on big leaves. Every member of the family gets their share and speedily devours it, lying on the ground picking up the food with their fingers.

After the meal the chief showed us his large potato and wheat fields, his pigs and his wonderful horses. The natives are passionately fond of riding and keep beautiful horses but they don't want to sell any of them. The prices they ask are so exorbitant (£150) as to make all dealing impossible. Even the women love riding, and in Wellington you see the wives and daughters of the chiefs on horseback, clad in European habits.

We now went, or rather crept, into the hut of the ordinary natives. The entrance was so narrow and low that we had to lie down flat and then crawl through. Inside we noticed half a dozen pigs, some dogs and three or four children lying about in peaceful unity. A fire was burning in the middle: the only escape for the rising smoke was the door. The Māori children wore only red or white blankets, and they had no scruples about throwing them off altogether when it began to get hot. They are shy of water and consequently very dirty; they teem with fleas and lice and unfortunately let us have a good share of them too.

Nearly all Māori are Christians; most are Protestants, although some tribes are Catholics. Since their conversion, polygamy has been abolished. The tattooing of children has also stopped, except for the lips of the girls, which is done to prevent the lips getting withered when the girls grow old.[13]

The women have an inferior position and are badly treated. They marry very early and then have to do all the hardest work, either in the fields or rooting up trees and splitting wood, while the men do nothing, or idle about on their horses. Yet the Māori are intelligent and quick-witted. In Auckland there are schools for Māori, and a newspaper—*Karere o Pōneke*—is published in their language.[14] All Māori are quite well off. They keep a lot of pigs, have horses and a few cows, and grow their own potatoes and corn. They are self-sufficient and never think of going into town to look for work.

Māori horse race on the Ruamahanga Plain, Wairarapa, 1852.

WOOD ENGRAVING FROM *ILLUSTRATED LONDON NEWS*

Ruamahanga River in south Wairarapa, circa 1863.

WATERCOLOUR AND CHINESE WHITE PAINTING
BY CHARLES DECIMUS BARRAUD

By giving them small presents we soon succeeded in winning their confidence, and when we said goodbye there was no end to their nose-rubbings and mutterings. We had no adventures on our way back. We arrived in Wellington on February 9th, very tired but perfectly well.

This excursion had given us so much pleasure we undertook a second one, leaving on February 14th. Again we were on horseback but this time without guides. We were accompanied by Major W, with whom we had travelled on the *Equator*.[15] Once more we rose through wonderful bush and rich valleys, passing farmsteads with flocks of sheep and cattle, the latter often very wild.

On the second day we arrived at Kaiwharawhara,[16] the aim of our trip. This is a small settlement inhabited only by natives, charmingly situated in a valley. The river that flows through it goes into a hot lake. Under the intelligent and vigorous leadership of their chief Te Wherowhero[17] (The Red One) the natives are in every way more advanced. They own very fine wheat and potato fields, pigs and cattle, and excellent horses. However, their whare are just as miserable as those we saw before, if somewhat cleaner as the warm lake is not far away. They love bathing there, just as much as they detest washing with cold water.

We introduced ourselves to the chief, who was squatting contentedly on the floor of his whare. He rose and received us with a 'Tena koe'—'Welcome'—and as he stretched out his arm to shake hands we luckily escaped the nose-rubbing. This chief is

Three Māori, two men and one woman, riding on horseback,
New Plymouth, 1856.

PENCIL AND WASH DRAWING BY WILLIAM STRUTT

powerfully built, six feet tall and aged between forty and forty-five. His face was heavily tattooed, his eyes very expressive, his teeth like ivory. Two shark's teeth dangled from his ears and he wore European clothes. His dwelling was furnished with common European household utensils. As he spoke English tolerably well, our conversation flowed merrily. His wife was working in the fields, and his daughter, Pōmare, was out riding.

After we had rested for a short time the chief offered to show us his people's huts and fields. We then strolled along to have a look at the hot lake, which has an extent of two miles. The surroundings were perfect. Beautiful vegetation blossomed right down to the bank. Thousands of wild ducks had found refuge. The picturesque wild fowl, with their brilliant colours of green and bronze, white breasts, and red beaks and feet, flew up with wild screechings when we came near them, and the parrots followed their example.

All of a sudden we heard the sound of an approaching horse. When the rider came into view we were amazed to see a beautiful Māori girl sitting perfectly on her horse—the chief's daughter. We never would have thought it possible that a native could be so handsome: our former experiences had not led us to expect anything so dazzling. She wore a black European habit. Her hat was also black, trimmed with red and blue feathers. Her features were as clear, as regular as those of a white woman, and not disfigured by tattooing, her colour a light brown, or rather yellow, her eyes and hair raven black. In her small mouth her teeth glistened like ivory.

'Tena koe,' she called out when she came nearer, and with wonderful lightness she jumped off her horse. We were greeting her in our best manner, but she got hold of the major's head and the nose-rubbing and mutterings were performed in great style, then H and I also got our share. I am sure this beautiful girl would find a European husband if it were not known that one had to marry her whole tribe at the same time. With her dowry of land, pigs, dogs, horses and potatoes—the amount according to the wealth of her father—she would be obliged to be hostess to the whole tribe for two months after her wedding, and to feed them on potatoes and bacon.

Unfortunately, the beautiful Pōmare could not speak English, but with her father she remained with us all the time. When the sun was setting the Māori went bathing. Old and young, men and women, disported themselves in the warm water, singing and screeching in unison with the squawking ducks. When this was over we ate a meal with our host but did not accept his invitation to stay the night, instead riding in the light of a full moon fifteen miles to the next inn.

I could fill pages and pages describing this interesting trip but I do not have the time. I will mention only that besides the beautiful bush there are many acres of land that produce only scrub. They are covered in manuka, flax and cabbage trees. The leaves of the manuka, if dried, make quite good tea, but on account of the high cost of labour it would not pay to cultivate it.

The flax is a beautiful plant belonging to the Liliaceae family and grows into a big shrub. The fibre of the leaves possesses great strength; the natives use it for their garments, and make ropes and a variety of other things with it. Unfortunately, all attempts have so far failed to extricate from the leaves a gummy substance that is an obstacle to using it more extensively for manufacturing, but without doubt some day science will find a remedy and New Zealand will be enriched with another article for export.

E Rangi and E Tohi of Port Nicholson Pa with Kiko,
an old woman of Tiakiwai kāinga, 1844.

WATERCOLOUR BY GEORGE FRENCH ANGAS

✣ ✣ ✣

Our life in Wellington has shaped itself much to our liking. Our highly respected friend Miss H, who was our travelling companion on the *Equator* and who came here to spend some time in this warm climate,[18] has given us the very best recommendations to all the best families. We have been invited to many dinners, breakfast parties and picnics, the latter always undertaken on horseback. I don't think there is a lady here who doesn't understand the art of riding.

The weather is wonderful just now, not too hot. We often have rain during the night. It is said there is a little earthquake nearly every week, but so far I have felt none. Thunderstorms happen very seldom, perhaps only one in the year, but the wind is often very strong. A few days ago, for instance, a boat lying on the shore was picked up and carried along a whole street length.

The peaches and grapes are ripe but very dear. So are the apples. In the garden of Mrs Edwards, the proprietor of our boarding house,[19] the apple trees are blooming for the second time. I have seen fuchsias which grow into regular trees. As a rule the house fronts are completely covered with them: only the windows shine through the foliage. One finds many of our indoor plants here in the gardens in luxurious magnificence; only the dahlias remain small and crippled. The weeping willow has been introduced to New Zealand from the Cape.

I have already collected a great many shells for Ernst Boll. You find them in great numbers on the beach: instead of sand there are shells and snails. I have found the same specimens inland at an altitude of about 2,000 to 3,000 feet—a sign of how considerable, even in the present geological period, the

Willis Street businesses south of the junction with Lambton Quay, 1860s.

PHOTOGRAPHER UNKNOWN

elevation of this volcanic island must have been—but I have not been able to find any fossils.

There are a good many Germans here. Travelling German artists even recently gave performances in the Wellington theatre.[20] Of our seamen in the *Equator*, six have deserted and more will follow their example. One cannot blame these poor fellows as they earn more money here in one week than they do in one month at sea. The English seamen follow the same practice and our captain is now forced to pay his men £7.8/– per month, instead of £1.10/–, for their dog's life on board.

March 18th

1859

Pioneer cottages, Cuba Street, Wellington, 1864.

PHOTOGRAPHER UNKNOWN

We are now in our own little rented cottage.[21] As servants are too expensive we do our own housekeeping, even the buying and cooking. All provisions are very dear and although we take only two meals a day our weekly expenses come to about £2. The following prices are charged:

- A hundredweight of potatoes, 10/–
- 1 pound of beefsteak, sixpence
- 1 pound of veal or mutton, nine pence
- Butter, 1/4
- Onion, nine pence
- Tea, 3/–
- Coffee, 1/6
- Sugar, sixpence

For our milk supply we have bought a beautiful little goat for 3/–.

We are also now acquainted with earthquakes. When we were having breakfast the other morning, all of a sudden the table began to shake so the plates fell off it. The earthquake lasted about 50 to 60 seconds. The weather was perfectly clear and the atmosphere showed nothing of an unusual nature. That same evening and the following days about every four hours

WELLINGTON INDEPENDENT, APRIL 19TH

ATTENTION!—SILENCE AND TREMBLE, for now rules the almighty George Augustus Selwyn, president of the Synod, Metropolitan Bishop of New Zealand, Melanesia, and God knows of what other parts of this earth besides! He is indeed a man of majestic appearance, slender, his eyes flashing, his features well-shaped, only rather too severe, with a chin that indicates most clearly that side of his character which is known as the most conspicuous one—his friends call it firmness, his adversaries stubbornness. He is a perfect master in all the arts of oratory. He possesses the supreme power of speech and is never at a loss for a word, though very often for the proof of it. He considers himself as a sort of species of Anglican Pope, born to rule, except his own passions. He could sit for the portrait of a Great Inquisitor. He does not lower himself to arguments, but he knows how to deal out blows with thundering voice and words. If the reasoning of an adversary is too difficult to confute, this presuming individual is crushed by the remark 'It is below the dignity of my office to take any notice of this.' The bishop has an income of £6,000 a year; he owns a small ship, undertakes trips to the Islands in her, and brings back sixteen to thirty young men, who are educated at his expense at Auckland, and after two years' training are sent back to their homeland.[22]

George Augustus Selwyn,
Anglican Bishop of New Zealand, circa 1869.

PHOTOGRAPH BY FRED WHITLOCK

we felt small shakes; these are more or less welcome as they are supposed to guard us from a major calamity.[23]

At present it is very lively in Wellington. A meeting of all New Zealand's Protestant clergy has been summoned by the bishop of Auckland. We hear that among them are ten to fifteen German missionaries, and also that the Catholic and Protestant missionaries have many quarrels, especially in the interior of the island. The Protestants try to get those tribes which were converted to the Roman church over to their side, and vice versa.

Some of the chiefs have been so angry about these disputes over religious doctrine that they have driven out both parties and reverted to their old heathenish customs. There are about thirteen churches of the different Christian confessions in the New Zealand isles.

✜ ✜ ✜

Yesterday we attended a sitting at the Court House, where a Māori was accused of theft. The scene was most interesting, although we understood not a word of the proceedings. Instead of engaging a lawyer, the plaintiff and accused were both represented by their chiefs, and these two arranged the matter between them and fixed the penalty.[24] The chiefs were accompanied by the whole of their respective tribes, including women and children, and the noise they made was so deafening you could not hear yourself speak.

When we were on a visit to the Hutt, where the natives occupy themselves greatly with fishing and eel-catching, we were interested to see their canoes. These were from 26 to 65 feet long and made from the single trunk of a tree, the prows ornamented with the most beautiful carving.

Paddlers in waka on the Hutt River being
greeted by Māori on the riverbank, 1847.

DRAWING BY SAMUEL CHARLES BREES;
ENGRAVING BY HENRY MELVILLE

April 14th

1859

View from the hill above Pukerua Bay out to Kāpiti Island on Taua-Tapu
track, and below to coastal route north, circa 1845.

DRAWING BY SAMUEL CHARLES BREES;
ENGRAVING BY HENRY MELVILLE

n the fourth of this month we set out for another trip into the interior. This time we went on foot. We were accompanied by Mr M, one of the scientists of whom I spoke in my last letter. He has studied philosophy, chemistry and jurisprudence, and is much thought of here. The government has appointed him to do scientific research work in the Wellington district.

As we were convinced of the peaceful character of the natives we did not take any weapons with us, but we soon had cause to regret this. An hour after our departure five criminals in Wellington gaol escaped after murdering the warder in broad daylight.[25] This, of course, made the woods very unsafe and we soon heard of burglaries, housebreaking and robberies. Although troops were sent out to pursue them and a reward of £10 to £50 was promised for their arrest, only three had been recaptured.

On this trip I had the best opportunity to admire the wonderful natural beauties of the country. On both earlier excursions the guiding of my horse, unused to riding as I was, had claimed too much of my attention. Now I could look at leisure upon the

Kāpiti and Mana Islands, with Cook Strait beyond, circa 1855.

WATERCOLOUR AND INK DRAWING BY JOHN PEARSE

magnificent trees, the charming brooks and their sources, the birds with their lovely coloured plumage. We were enchanted by the many wonders of our surroundings. Mr M remarked that the thing that gave New Zealand such a particular attraction was the freshness of the green in which the trees were clad through all the seasons. In New Holland,[26] India and the South Sea Isles the great heat burns up the leaves of the trees and for months you see no fresh green. Although it was now autumn here, you might think it was spring. There is a great variety in the green of the trees: from the very lightest they shade down to the very darkest of colouring.

It was six o'clock in the evening when we arrived in Porirua but the goal we had set ourselves was still further away, and against all warnings of the inhabitants we walked on. We might have had to pay dearly for this, for the road from Porirua winds itself along a bay which is passable everywhere at low tide, but at high tide is passable only for people thoroughly acquainted with the locality. Soon we were up to our knees in the water. When it continued to rise higher and higher we were forced to retrace our steps, and as it was now dark we had great difficulty finding the right road.

When at last we saw a house we went up and knocked, but the door was not opened. We then asked, 'How far is it to the next inn?' and were told it was another two miles. We now continued to walk in that direction but the people who lived in the house suspected us of being the escaped prisoners. They ran after us and began firing, and when they caught up to us they bound our hands and feet in spite of our angry protestations. Resistance was useless and would only have endangered our position.

We felt sure the misunderstanding would be cleared up the next day but this happened sooner than we would have thought possible. We were taken into a nearby house and luckily there was a sergeant who recognised Mr M and apologised. 'But,' he said, 'it really is your own fault, for in this country one does not travel after sun is down, especially not on foot. I have to ask you to discontinue this practice in future.'

We were now conducted to the inn where the host, not trusting such latecomers, also received us with an axe and a revolver, for he too believed we were the escaped prisoners. When a similar outbreak had occurred some time ago he had been robbed by one of the fugitives, who took possession of his schooner and slipped away in her as far as Nelson, where he was recaptured.

On the next morning we set out again and walked along the bay at low tide. Situated in the bay there are some small islands.[27] A great number of canoes paddled by the natives lent a charming animation to the pretty scene.

After a four-mile walk we left the beach behind us and entered the bush, and very gradually, hardly realising it, we climbed a 3,000-foot-high mountain.[28] From the summit we had a simply magnificent view, especially as it was clear and the sun was setting. Mr M declared that in no part of the globe had he seen a more beautiful view. Before us was the sea, smooth as a mirror and of a heavenly blue. Out of its depth rose the island of Kāpiti, her mountains glowing like fire under the rays of the setting sun. And still further away, on the far horizon, we saw the high mountains of the South Island covered with snow. To the north we could follow the line of the beach for about 60 to 80 miles, while in the north-east the high mountains of our island were visible.

Paekākāriki hill road, looking out to Kāpiti Island, 1877.

PENCIL AND WATERCOLOUR DRAWING BY CHARLES DECIMUS BARRAUD

Group of Māori and Pākehā at Paekākāriki, with travellers
on the beach road, circa 1845.

WATERCOLOUR BY SAMUEL CHARLES BREES

And spreading out from the sea to the foot of the mountain lay the most beautiful valley, called Paekākāriki. As we looked down on it, the whare of the Māori resembled small birds' nests, and descending down to it we became more and more aware of its marvels and variety.

Here we stopped for two days, meeting only one white man during that time, an Englishman who had studied jurisprudence in Cambridge but had now nearly become a native himself. Very soon the friendliest relations were established between the Māori and ourselves: any amount of nose-rubbing took place, we presented them with pipes and tobacco, strolled through their plantations of maize, shooed away the thieving parrots, inspected their cattle and rode their horses. Full of curiosity, the children followed us everywhere. They were mostly naked or wore a torn rag supposed to be a shirt. All this was so unusual I felt as if I had been transported into fairyland.

At the beach I gathered a rich harvest of shells. I even found a Trochus imperialis, although incomplete. The perfect ones are such a rarity that Bishop Selwyn has promised a reward of £2 for faultless specimens.

From Paekākāriki we walked along the beach to Waikanae, where nine years ago a battle was fought between Māori and the British troops.[29] You still saw the remnants of the whare partially destroyed by the firing, and also the altars where white people had been butchered.[30] Two poles about 40 feet high stood at the side, the points decorated with hideous-looking carved figures. Bones and skulls had been collected in small heaps and were covered with shells.

Trochus imperialis, 'such a rarity that Bishop Selwyn has
promised a reward of £2 for faultless specimens', 1859.

ENGRAVING FROM *ILLUSTRATED NATURAL HISTORY OF THE ANIMAL KINGDOM*

Waikanae is the starting place for Kāpiti. It was our intention
to visit the island (in a canoe) but as the sea was very rough we
felt it was not safe to trust our lives to such a frail-looking craft,
so we wandered further along the coast to Ōtaki and amused
ourselves watching the procedure by which the birds caught
their food. Thousands and thousands of gulls and other sea-
birds dip down into the water to catch mussels. They are too
hard for them to crack, so they take their prey high up into the
air and drop them from there. The shell is then opened and,
like hawks, with lightning speed they swoop down and greed-
ily devour this titbit. We really had to laugh at this sight: it was
truly funny to see thousands of birds always make exactly the
same movement.

Nikau palms in the Wellington region, circa 1848–1860.

WATERCOLOUR BY CHARLES EMILIUS GOLD

We now reached the Ōtaki River where, with its five arms, it flows into the sea. The sun was setting in glorious colours, and after having rowed across the river we came to one of the most delightful places I have ever beheld. The fertile plain through which the Ōtaki River flows is shaped in a semicircle. On one side is the sea. On the other it is surrounded by high mountains. The snow in the deep fissures and on the summit lit up by the last rays of the sinking sun seemed to be a blaze of fire. The soil was covered with fine grass and we found an enormous number of mushrooms growing on it. Thousands of beautiful nikau palms and huge bushes of acacias stood about in single groups. The scene was enlivened by herds of pigs, cattle and horses, all of whom jumped up and ran away when we came near.

After a two-hour walk through the valley we reached Ōtaki, the biggest native settlement in the province of Wellington and at a distance of 55 English miles from the capital. The place was laid out by English engineers and the plan greatly resembles the star-shaped design of Neustrelitz:[31] from the centre you look into all the different streets. Its population consists of 800 to 1,000 Māori and about 60 white people; the latter are mostly farmers, or traders and missionaries.[32] They all speak the native language as well as their own. The Māori are all well-to-do and fairly civilised; many wear old European clothes and their dwellings are somewhat cleaner than those I saw on my former trips. The outsides of their whare look rather pretty. Each dwelling is enclosed by acacias and peach trees, and a crop of potatoes and maize stands in the ground. We wanted to see the inside of their huts and a very humorous Irishman who was working there and who spoke Māori was made our leader and interpreter.

The visits we paid to the chiefs, Mātene Te Whiwhi and Tamihana Te Rauparaha,[33] were the most interesting. Both men had dwellings according to their rank, and these included appointments of European luxury; there are no better ones to be seen in Wellington. The house of Mātene Te Whiwhi is situated in a garden, but on both sides you perceived the miserable abodes of his subordinate servants. A verandah covered with a beautiful green creeper runs along the whole front of the house. The walls of the large entrance hall are decorated with a sort of wickerwork done in toi toi grass, divided into sections by long carved staves. A costly lamp hangs from the ceiling.

When we entered the reception room we saw old Martin sitting on a sofa. He gave us his hand as a token of welcome, but as he could not speak English the conversation had to be carried

Mātene Te Whiwhi, Ngāti Toa and
Ngāti Raukawa leader, at Ōtaki, circa 1870.

on by our Irishman. The room was furnished in very good taste. A beautiful carpet lay on the floor and the coverings of the chairs, armchairs and sofa were of the finest green Morocco leather. The seats were grouped around a large mahogany table, on which were heaped books in English and Māori. There was also an inkstand and some other dainty-looking utensils. Portraits of Queen Victoria, Prince Albert, the Prince of Wales and Napoleon, all in fine copperplate, hung on the walls, as well as an oil painting of the chief himself. Specimens of fossils from Lake Taupō, the waters of which have healing qualities, stood on the mantelpiece.

A young serving girl appeared and offered us apples as refreshment. Although Martin possesses this wonderful house he cannot bear to live in it; he goes back to his whare and only there feels happy and at home. His ambition to be the owner of a house in European style has been satisfied and that is enough for him.

Tamihana Te Rauparaha, having the same name as his father, who was dreaded by the British for his cannibalism, is a very handsome young man, not tattooed. In the battle of Waikanae he was taken prisoner, subsequently sent to England, lived there for three years, and received a first-class education. Now he is back and rules his tribe judiciously. The white people hate him as he is too clever for them: he won't let himself be gulled like the other chiefs.

We had a long conversation with him. He recognises the failings of his people and tries to civilise them, but he said Māori imagine themselves to be the cleverest people on Earth. 'When I speak to them about England and London they don't believe a thing and say I have been paid to try and make them believe

Tamihana Te Rauparaha, son of Ngāti Toa chief
Te Rauparaha, during his visit to London, 1852.

Tamihana Te Rauparaha's house at Ōtaki, built in a combined Māori and Pākehā style.

WATERCOLOUR BY CHARLES EMILIUS GOLD

in my tales.' His house is even more sumptuous than that of Mātene Te Whiwhi. He lives in it, although his family does not.

We saw an oil portrait of his father—a wild, dark face, tattooed all over. His cloak was interwoven with albatross feathers, sharks' teeth were hanging from his ears, and on his chest he was wearing the image of an idol as his talisman. He was holding a battle-axe in one hand and a greenstone club in the other.[34] This beautiful stone, which the Māori value as if it were gold, comes from the South Island. They wear it as ornaments on their breast or in their ears.

Ōtaki is full of activity just now. The natives have been holding a big meeting and twenty-one prominent chiefs have come with their attendants. The question of who was going to be elected as their king had to be settled and, as the old hoary Te Puni had declined to accept the glory, the chief Te Wherowhero was unanimously elected.[35]

Tamihana had the kindness to invite us and our Irishman to be his guests at the dinner which was going to be served to all the chiefs at two o'clock in the afternoon, so we took our seats at the festive board, which was laid in the usual English style. When I looked around and beheld the wild, dark faces I did feel far from home: it was a peculiar experience to take a meal in this extraordinary company.

It was amusing to watch their manners. They helped themselves to salt, pepper and mustard, and at first began eating by using their forks and knives. However, by and by the strange tools were discarded and put aside, and before we were halfway through our meal old customs were reverted to: fingers did service for taking up the food, Tamihana being the one exception.

Inside Rangiātea Church, Ōtaki, with Māori listening to a sermon
by Octavius Hadfield, circa 1850s or early 1860s.

LITHOGRAPH BY CHARLES DECIMUS BARRAUD;
HAND-COLOURED PRINTED CALICO BY UNKNOWN ARTIST

At four o'clock, after dinner, the whole Māori population of Ōtaki was assembled on a big open plot. The wives of all the chiefs made their appearance and either lay about on the grass or sat on their horses. The young ones, with only a shirt on, hopped about and performed a dance. They all stood in a row and moved their hands and right foot in a certain rhythm, which was repeated over and over again by all the dancers, with either the leader or the whole choir singing.

Our travelling companion, who wished to contribute his share to the entertainment, showed the chiefs different species of New Zealand wood through his microscope, and I only wish you could have witnessed their great astonishment. They expressed it in a long drawn-out cry, which lasted as long as they looked on this inconceivable wonder. At five o'clock the chiefs rode away, followed by their wives, also on horseback, and their male attendants, while the female attendants had to walk.

Here in Ōtaki there is a beautiful Māori church built of wood and reed.[36] The plain inner walls are covered with carving—tattoo-style, if I may express it like that. The altar consists of part of a tree trunk and is enclosed by a railing; both also display rich and beautiful carving. No pew, no seat, is to be found as the Māori, according to their custom, sit on the ground.

We visited the preacher, a young Māori in a black coat with a white band around his neck.[37] He showed us the school and the institution where the children are taught both practical and theoretical agriculture. We also had a look at the Catholic church that is being erected and promises to be a fine building.[38] Many Māori here belong to the Roman church. They also have a great liking for the French—the 'Oui Ouis', as they call them.

Carved altar rails, tukutuku panels, and part of the inscription
'Ko Ahau Te Huarahi, Te Pono, Me Te Ora' ('I am the way, the truth
and the life') in Rangiātea Church.

PHOTOGRAPH BY ALBERT PERCY GODBER

We also heard that a young German doctor named Rothe had lived here for some years. Worshipped by the natives, he married a Māori girl and had two sons, but a month ago he and his horse were drowned in an attempt to swim through the Rangitikei River. He was deeply mourned by the whole population but nobody could tell me from what part of Germany he originated.

On the morning of the 11th we started on our return journey but Mr M remained behind as he wanted to make another trip from Ōtaki. We travelled back by the same road we came and our Irishman accompanied us right down to Wellington.

I have told you of the great pleasure this trip has been to me. I must now mention some of the discomforts that were connected with it. These consisted chiefly in the onslaught of various insects. We were mercilessly tormented by mosquitoes, sandflies and fleas, H and I being the worst sufferers, while Mr M was not touched by them. He told us they were far more poisonous in Australia and India, so we were lucky after all.

May 25th

1859

Corner of Cuba and Ghuznee Streets, Wellington, including premises of
Kirkcaldie & Stains, General Drapers, circa 1860s.

PHOTOGRAPHER UNKNOWN

ere in Wellington there are quite a number of families whose means would not be sufficient for them to play a prominent part in English society, equal to the way of life expected of a person of rank. But these very people make the best colonists and take first place as their income is enough for them to buy a nice property and keep a carriage, groom and horses. You find, therefore, a good many men who have left the English army and settled on the land. When they enter the country they get a donation from the government of a thousand acres at 10/- or a smaller piece of land in town to the value of £500.

Immigration into New Zealand increases all the time and for very good reason: every worker and craftsman can make a very good living here and be in an independent position in a very short time. Among the seamen who deserted from our ship, the *Equator*, are a painter, a shoemaker and a carpenter. These people manage to save about 35 shillings a week, which they hand over to us in trust every Saturday. They get £2 a week from their employers, for which they work only eight hours a day. Their board costs them about £1 per week and they make this money by working in their free time.

The climate is good and very healthy, there are no direct taxes, and everybody has the right to free thought and free speech. Everyone finds work and those who don't get on have only themselves to blame. The Swedish seamen knew no English when they arrived but now speak it fairly well, and as they are good workers and thrifty they hope to save from £80 to £90 a year. If these circumstances were known in my fatherland many young men would take advantage of them. Even if the voyage costs them £30 they can pay that off within a year.

Artisans, especially joiners, carpenters, tailors, painters, glaziers, shoemakers, saddlers and cooks, are the best paid. Farm labourers are able to save from 15 to 20 shillings a week without any difficulty. Of course they have to be sober, orderly and industrious. The married labourer is often better off than the single worker, especially if he has a wife who is capable and active, because when the husband works away from home she can earn nearly as much as he does. For laundry, for instance, she can charge at least three shillings for every twelve pieces. A young married couple also has a chance to work for a farmer in the interior who will pay them £50 to £60 a year and provide them with all other necessities. However, this is not the country for young men belonging to aristocratic families. They would not find a suitable occupation—unless they wanted to farm, in which case they would require at least £600 to invest in land.

There is a great deal of money to be made from ready cash. You get at least ten percent on your capital with good security, and those who know the run of the ropes can make from 20 to 25 percent. H and I have thought of investing a small sum into sheep every year. You hand them over to a farmer who takes care of them and receives a third of the lambs and the wool. If you buy a few more sheep every year you can soon have a nice flock as the percentage of lambing is very high. The merchants who live here make this sort of investment for every child of theirs; at the age of twenty they will be the owners of flocks amounting to 5,000 to 10,000 sheep.

The evenings are beginning to be very long now. The sun goes down at five o'clock and rises again at 7.15 a.m. The winter days are an hour longer than yours at home, while in summer they are an hour shorter. The weather at present is very fine and does not resemble the German November season. The fuchsias in front of the house are in full bloom and the acacias look fresh and vigorous. Fruit trees and all other trees are clad in green foliage. It rains for perhaps a day or two and the wind often reaches gale force, but after that we have had real summer weather, simply beautiful. The sky is a truly heavenly blue and when the sun goes down the colouring over the sea and on the mountains is really magnificent. Living in these beautiful surroundings one should never feel unhappy.

Lately there has been much life and activity here as Governor Browne came to buy land from the natives.[39]

The district through which I have been travelling, the peaceful, lovely valley of Paekākāriki, is now in possession of the government.[40] The natives whose hospitality we enjoyed are not there any more—with their families and all their goods and belongings they have gone north to the warm lakes. In a single year their land, now belonging to white people, will be completely changed, therefore I am very pleased to have still seen it in its original state.

✜ ✜ ✜

The following statistical and political notes may be of some interest to you. The northern island is subdivided into four provinces—Auckland, Hawke's Bay, New Plymouth and Wellington—and the southern island into three, namely Nelson, Canterbury and Otago. The number of colonists, excluding the military force, amounted to 49,738 in the year 1857. The following year there was an increase of 9,565 in the white population.

The livestock were as follows:

1857	1858
1,051,374 sheep	1,523,316 sheep
106,502 cattle	137,188 cattle
10,589 horses	14,912 horses

The area of New Zealand is estimated at 70 million acres,[41] of which half is suitable for cultivation. Last year only 140,946 acres were under the plough for grain, maize and potato growing, and another 235,468 had been fenced in.

Auckland is the seat of the governor—at present His Excellency Colonel Thomas Gore Browne—who is nominated by the Queen. Each province has its special superintendent, with two ministers elected by the people, but every law issued by the provincial government has to be first ratified by the governor.

There are two political factions, the radicals and the constitutionals. The first has the largest number of adherents and is against the government; the second is composed of followers of

Thomas Robert Gore Browne, governor of New Zealand 1855–1861,
with his wife, daughter, son and private secretary, circa 1859.

PHOTOGRAPH BY JOHN NICOL CROMBIE

Wellington Provincial Council building, circa 1858.

PHOTOGRAPH BY GEORGE HENRY SWAN

the governor. Nearly all the provincial superintendents, except those of Nelson and Canterbury, are radicals. This leads to a great many disputes as the provincial radicals are jealous of the central government[42] and fight against it. Each party has its own paper (in Wellington alone there are three of them),[43] in which they attack each other in the most rude and barefaced manner.

Because of these jealousies the governor received a very cool reception in Wellington. As our superintendent belongs to the radicals, the governor found more favour with the farmers, while the natives approached him with the greatest reverence: every one of them wanted to see the 'Kovanah', as they called him. Several hundred had come to town, on horseback or on foot, accompanied by their women. It was a marvellous sight to see these old tattooed figures on their horses holding spear and battle-axe in their hands. The women wore half European riding outfits. I saw, for instance, one in a sweeping velvet habit, bare-headed, and with a clay pipe between her lips.

I have already mentioned the warm lakes and will tell you a little more about this. Nearly all Māori who can manage it go every year to the hot baths at Lake Taupō. The distance from here is about 235 miles. There is no road yet, not even a track for riding, and the few Europeans who go have to join a caravan of natives—which is already necessary for their safety, as there are many wild, quite uncivilised tribes in the interior who are hostile to white people.

The lake, with a number of hot springs, is supposed to be a most beautiful sight. One of the geysers reaches a height of 60

Hot pools at Tokaanu near Lake Taupō, 1844.

WATERCOLOUR BY GEORGE FRENCH ANGAS

Twin geyser, Wairakei, 1886.

OIL PAINTING BY CHARLES BLOMFIELD

feet when it spouts. Everything put into its water is soon covered with a sort of incrustation; we saw a lot of samples—plants, shells and other objects—on Mātene Te Whiwhi's mantelpiece in Ōtaki.

The government has now decided to make a road to Taupō. We shall then know more about this lake than what the Māori tell you, although we are bound to get some information from Dr Hochstetter as the Auckland papers report he is travelling in that region.

Honiana Te Puni-kokopu seated in a whare on the shore of
Wellington Harbour, probably at Pito-one (Petone), 1860.

WATERCOLOUR BY CHARLES DECIMUS BARRAUD

Now I must tell you of some of the characteristics of the native people as they strike me. They always think first of their own profit and never do anything without looking for an equivalent: I believe if a Māori had the chance to save a person from drowning, he would first make sure of the price for the rescue. On the other hand one can easily make friends of them by giving them small gifts.

When we returned from Paekākāriki we were overtaken on the road by old Te Puni, who was driving in a trap. He is a very high-class Māori chief who lives at the Hutt.[44] He was accompanied by a boy and ten attendants on horseback, and was returning from a wedding at Waikanae. Our Irishman did a deal with him, asking him to take his swag to the next inn. For rendering this service we would give him 1/6. When we arrived the old chief was still there. We ordered our meal and the Irishman asked him to join us, which he was quite willing to do as long as we paid for him. We did not feel inclined to comply with this demand as he is supposed to be a rich man with an estate worth £10,000.

The Irishman began to give high praise to the food, which was served to us while Te Puni sat there as a greedy onlooker, seemingly counting every morsel we ate. At last he got up and put a shilling on the table, telling the Irishman he could have that shilling if he would pay for his dinner. As a further inducement he offered to take the swag another four miles further on.

This scene made a painful impression on me. I pitied this very old man, who was at one time one of New Zealand's mightiest chiefs and who, only quite lately, had refused the honour of being king to his people. He had been born in freedom in this country, which was once his very own. Now he stood there, humiliated by the white man. Te Puni used to have a bad reputation on account of his excessive cannibalism—he was notorious for the orgies of butcheries he committed—but for many years he has been a warm friend to the white people. In recent wars he has saved hundreds who would otherwise have been killed; as a reward the government allows him a yearly pension of £50.

We gave him two glasses of beer, which unfortunately made him very drunk—so much so that he missed a turning in the road and drove right into the sea. The trap capsized and he was thrown out and wounded on his head. We washed the blood off him and from this time on he has been a great friend. He comes now and again to see us in Wellington and always invites us to visit him. He told us that according to Māori law we deserved to be killed, for whenever you touch the head of a chief—for whatever reason it may be—it means death to the offender.[45]

We also made the acquaintance of another ill-reputed cannibal named Pairuruck.[46] He was in the service of Tamihana Te Rauparaha's father, by whose orders he is supposed to have slaughtered 500 Māori of a hostile tribe. The most revolting occurrence was the slaughtering of a young Māori girl who was his slave. Several Europeans witnessed this ghastly cruelty but were unable to come to her assistance. The unfortunate girl was sent out to collect wood, which was going to be used for the cooking of her own body. After she had done this, he stabbed her and drank her warm blood. Now he has turned to the Protestant religion but is still the bugbear of all children: mothers use his name to frighten and silence them when they are naughty.

The Māori have peculiar ways in their dealings. When they come into town with their pigs, fish, potatoes and flax, they first go and have a meal and nothing is allowed to interfere with this, be there ever so many buyers. At eleven o'clock they have finished and are ready for business, but if they can't get the price they have set on their goods they would rather take them back than accept a lower price.

At about two o'clock they assemble at an appointed place, and under the leadership of their chief thirty or forty of them, including women and children, begin to visit the shops to make their purchases. An instance is a woollen blanket. If there should be fifty of these in a shop, each has to be shown and closely examined by the whole crowd. In the end the chief always chooses the article in question. After this discussions begin about the price, and if at last an agreement is reached they all walk off and go into the next shop. Here exactly the same scene takes place, and out of all the much-fingered wares the one that appears the cheapest is chosen. This means a real trial in patience for the shopkeepers.

Peace between Māori tribes has at last been restored, to everybody's great satisfaction—the scene of war was only about 80 miles from here.[47] The fear of an outbreak of hostilities between Māori and Pākehā has also been removed for the present.[48]

February 7th

1862

Nelson's port and wharf buildings, circa 1860.

left Wellington on January 24th and the following morning we sailed into Nelson Harbour. There I visited our correspondent Herr August Weyergang, a native of Lauenburg and brother-in-law of the merchant Carl Drewes in Wismar, who has been living in Nelson for six years.[49]...

As the steamer did not resume its journey on to Auckland until January 28th, I made use of the free time this left me by paying a visit, with Herr W as my guide, to the nearby Mecklenburg colony in Waimea. We rode out from Nelson early on Sunday morning (the 26th), and arrived about 8 a.m. at the home of Herr Fedor Kelling,[50] who had led settlement here eighteen years ago, and was the first German elected to the New Zealand parliament. His wife is now dead and his oldest daughter, who is about seventeen, takes care of the housework with the help of her fourteen-year-old sister, while his two sons, eighteen and fourteen, help their father with his work.

I was given the friendliest of welcomes and immediately felt at home. We looked at the meadows, the corn fields and the village, which has a thoroughly Mecklenburg stamp about it and is quite different from the settlements of the English colonists.

There was only one thing I did not see, namely the stork's nest up on the large barn!

After lunch we rode off to the various original settler families, whose children and grandchildren have all become related to each other by intermarriage and now form a sizeable community of some 400 persons. They all speak Plattdeutsch[51] and only a few are able to speak any English.

I can hardly describe with what joy I was received everywhere by these people. Inside their homes it looks just as it does in our homes back in Mecklenburg, the only difference being that more prosperity prevails here in the colony. Gaudy illustrated broadsheets depicting Christ's sufferings hang without frames on the wall, along with scenes of marriage and murder. The cuckoo clock is next to the stove, the large armchair sits in the corner, and the four-poster bed takes up a large space.

We first visited the Siggelkows, one of the oldest couples. They have seven married children, some of whom were visiting with the grandchildren. Here we had to drink coffee and eat bread—Stuten—but as we still had another four visits to make Kelling warned me to mind how much I ate: if we did not want to slight people we would have to enjoy something everywhere we went.

These people have all remained Mecklenburgers through and through in their manners and habits. ... You ought to have just seen, for instance, with what a satisfied look Old Mother Siggelkow poured coffee into the best cup for me until it almost overflowed, and how Fieken had to fetch white sugar for the gentleman from Mecklenburg so he could see for certain that they had it, and how he had to sample the rich layer of cream, and the Stuten that the innkeeper's wife had put aside for her from the christening ceremony.

German settler and Lutheran minister Johann Heine in his garden at
Upper Moutere, Nelson, 1880s.

Several generations of German settlers at the 50th wedding
anniversary of Reverend Johann Heine and his wife Anna (both seated
in high-backed chairs), probably Upper Moutere, 1899.
Fedor Kelling is in the second row, second from right, and his son,
Fedor Kelling Jr, in the centre of the back row.

PHOTOGRAPHER UNKNOWN

Before I left, Old Mother Siggelkow took me once more by the hand to show me her riches, and led me through the clean kitchen, well provided with shining cutlery, to the pantry, where sausages, hams and sides of bacon were hung, bowls of milk stood on the sideboards, and in a small pail of fresh water lay some eight to ten pounds of fresh butter, which I of course had to taste. Then she called her hens, ducks and turkeys, which, at the sound of her familiar voice, all came hurrying up. Next we went to the pigs, the cows and the horses, and finally to the barn, where the full fields of corn were shown to me through the loft window.

After we had finally returned to the main room, one of the grandsons had to fetch the large key to the trunk, which brought forth a great shout of joy among the little throng. The lid was unlocked and with unspeakable pride and joy on her face Old Mother Siggelkow unfolded her linen. She seemed to pride herself the most on this and began to give a long speech, the gist of which was that they were so rich that, like a landed gentleman in Mecklenburg, they did not need to go about on foot but could ride instead.

In the midst of this it occurred to her I had not yet seen the 'blackies', whereupon Karl was sent immediately to fetch both horses. In the meantime, the rumour that someone from Mecklenburg had arrived spread among the neighbours, who arrived with their families to say hello as well.

After this we paid a visit to the four clans of the Schröders, the Windelborns, the Fanselows and the Langes, where there was also no lack of a genuinely German spirit. Everyone remembers their homeland in Mecklenburg with affection of course, but nobody would like to go back there; old Herr Schröder said to me, 'If there were twenty horses harnessed up to my wagon, they wouldn't drag me back to Mecklenburg.' Things are going well for everyone. Anyone who wants to work has not only his daily bread but within a few years can establish a home of his own and become prosperous.

These people emigrated here in 1844 at the instigation of Count Kuno zu Rantzau-Breitenburg, whose wife belonged to the entailed estate of Neu-Bothmer at Klütz.[52] He sold them the land, which he had bought from the New Zealand Company and which consisted of seven allotments or sections, each at a purchase price of £300 sterling. Each section comprised 150 acres that lay further away from the coast, 50 acres in the Waimea Valley, and one acre in the town of Nelson, which at the time was just coming into being. Almost everyone has disposed of their outlying property and confined themselves to their property in the Waimea Valley. Foolishly, though, they have also sold their town plots, which have already risen greatly in value. I did not see Fedor Kelling's brother Carl:[53] his residence was some ten miles further on and I didn't have the time to go there.

In Auckland at the place of C. Petschler[54]—a Neubrandenburger who has been established as a merchant there for several years—I stumbled on a small library in which there was a whole series of Mecklenburg civil calendars, and Fritz Reuter's poems,[55] which even in Wellington are widely distributed among the Mecklenburgers. When I told them I knew the author personally, they shouted, 'How's that possible? Send our many greetings to the gentleman!'—which you can consider as having been done with pleasure. As a consequence of having this greeting passed on to him, Fritz Reuter has dispatched a copy of his complete works to the settlement as a gift.

Since July 1859 even the Rostock flag[56] has been blowing in New Zealand as the ship *Maria Rösner*, commanded by Captain Eggers and belonging to ship-owners from Rostock, arrived in Wellington Harbour. Since then it has been used to ship cargo between the various ports of the islands.[57]

Friedrich Krull in the uniform of Consul for the German Empire.
He was appointed in 1871 aged thirty-six.

Epilogue

———•———

S oon after their arrival in Wellington, the energetic and
enterprising Friedrich Krull and Karl Hartmann set up a
trading business, Krull & Co. Just over two years later—on July
3, 1861—Krull became Consul for Hamburg, having applied
through a Hamburg trading firm, Schultz & Pinckernelle, for the
position to be established in order to protect not only Hamburg
merchant ships and their captains but also the interests of
German immigrants and open trade between the two countries.
He became a naturalised New Zealander on September 1, 1862,
and over time his consular duties expanded. On July 16, 1868
he became Consul for the North German Confederation and on
August 25, 1871 Consul for the German Empire in Wellington,
appointed by Kaiser Wilhelm I.

Krull enjoyed an active life in Wellington's business and
political community and formed many lasting friendships.
He became director and then chairman of the board of the
Wellington Gas Company, a city councillor, and a founding
member of the Wellington Chamber of Commerce. He was
elected to the Wellington Harbour Board and served as a Justice
of the Peace.

Wellington viewed from the Post Office tower, circa 1880s.
The garden and gazebo of Friedrich Krull's Boulcott Street
house can be seen in the centre below the fire bell tower.

By 1878 he had accumulated an investment of £70,000, only
to lose it all when the City of Glasgow Bank failed spectacularly
in October that year; ironically, some of its poor investments
had been in New Zealand sheep farming and wool. He sold his
Wellington business in 1884 and moved to Whanganui, taking up
a partnership with a stock and station firm, Freeman R. Jackson,
in 1886. As a consequence of the move north he resigned from
his various posts, but due to his length of service and popularity

Friedrich Krull with his wife and family at their
home in Whanganui, early 1900s. The Krull family moved
to the town in 1884.

PHOTOGRAPHER UNKNOWN

the authorities refused to accept his resignation as German
consul and persuaded him to continue in office, even though
a suitable replacement would have to be found for Wellington.

When he was in his late seventies, Friedrich Krull was dev-
astated by the outbreak of the First World War. Three and a
half months after being informed that it was treasonous to
further communicate with Germany he died of a stroke on
November 28, 1914.

CHILDREN OF FRIEDRICH KRULL

Friedrich August Krull and his wife Keren Happuch Krull (née Murch) married in 1862 and are believed to have had eight children, six of whom survived into adulthood:

Charlotte Ellen Katherine (Lotte) (circa 1864–?).
Married John Smylie McDewell Thompson, 1884.

Marian Anna (Ernard) (1865–?).
Married Hugh Reginald Hearson, 1899.

Phillip Augustus (1867–1936).
Married Käthe Ahlers, 1900.

Keren Anna Louise (1870–?).
Married Albert Mahler, 1902.

Fritz (1874–1962).
Married Dorothy Edith Varnham, 1920.

Margarita Kate (Gretel) (1875–?).
Married Charles McKellar Strouts, 1911.

Awa Press welcomes all further information on the Krull family genealogy.

NOTES

January 27th, 1859

1. Cape of Good Hope.

2. Karl Hartmann.

3. Wellington was the New Zealand Company's first official settlement. An advance party arrived on September 20, 1839 and, despite the protests of Ngāti Toa chief Te Rauparaha, bought land from chiefs Te Puni-Kokopu of Pito-one and Te Wharepōuri of Ngauranga. Six ships soon followed, the first arriving on January 22, 1840. A settlement was established at Pito-one (now Petone) at the north end of the harbour but flooding was a problem and a new settlement was launched on the site of present-day Wellington, despite the fact that many local Māori had not been party to any land sale and those who were remained in the dark as to the meaning of what they had signed.

4. By 1858 the European population of New Zealand had reached approximately 60,000, outnumbering the Māori population for the first time across the country as a whole (although not yet in the North Island). However, alienation of land in Wellington—serious flaws in the original purchase exposed

by Commissioner William Spain in 1842 were subsequently overlooked by the Crown in favour of a process of awarding additional compensation to Māori in return for extinguishment of their claims to ownership—coupled with an earthquake in 1855 that raised land and so destroyed marine food sources, meant many Māori had left the area. Some returned to their tribal homelands in Taranaki to settle land disputes.

February 25th, 1859

5. Ferdinand von Hochstetter, a German geologist, had arrived in New Zealand on December 22, 1858 on the *Novara*, a ship carrying out scientific research around the globe. Persuaded to stay on, he and fellow German Julius Haast carried out extensive geological surveys before Hochstetter returned to Europe a year later.

6. People who had stayed on at Pito-one had had to cope with regular flooding. In 1855 a large earthquake had sent a tsunami up the Hutt River but also drained some of the lower river valley.

7. Ponga or silver fern; botanical name Cyathea dealbata.

8. Kākāriki, yellow- and red-crowned and orange-fronted parakeets, were once plentiful throughout New Zealand but are now largely confined to a few offshore islands. Their demise on the mainland was caused by the clearing of forest, predation by introduced rats and stoats, and shooting and trapping by farmers protecting grain and fruit crops.

9. An Arms Importation Ordinance introduced in 1845, along with a further Arms Ordinance the following year, had prohibited the sale of firearms to Māori.

10. Possibly Angus McMaster at Tuhitarata, one of the first five sheep stations in the Wairarapa.

11. Early traders and missionaries, and latterly speculators in New South Wales, initially bought land directly from Māori. Sales stepped up when it appeared the British government was going to declare sovereignty over New Zealand. On January 14, 1840, New South Wales governor George Gipps issued a proclamation forbidding future land sales except to the Crown. When William Hobson arrived in Waitangi as British Consul on January 30 he issued a similar edict. On February 6 the Treaty of Waitangi was signed by around 50 Māori chiefs, who gave the Crown sole right to buy their lands. The Treaty's provision on land sales was to be much honoured in the breach. Māori disillusionment and anger would lead to the New Zealand Wars of 1845 to 1872. However, Krull appears mistaken on this occasion as there were no such private purchases in the Wairarapa. The farmer had more likely leased the land informally from Māori prior to 1853, when the first wave of Crown purchasing commenced in the district. The Crown's exclusive right of purchase was abolished after 1862 and Krull himself, in 1873, purchased from Māori two Wairarapa blocks near Te Ore Ore, covering a total area of 4,726 acres.

12. The identity of this pa and Te Turuatakiti are not known. There were many kainga of Ngāti Hāmua along the Ruamahanga River.

13. In fact it was never customary for children to receive tā moko; the process commenced at about the age of puberty for both males and females.

14. Published in Wellington by Walter Buller, the paper lasted for some fourteen months before ceasing publication.

15. A Major Wood is listed among the passengers who sailed to Wellington with Krull.

16. The identity of this settlement, the warm lake and the chief and his family is a mystery. It is possible the lake was in the Taupō volcanic zone, perhaps Lake Rotokawa, a well-known refuge of wild fowl, Lake Rotoaira, where early travellers reported a Māori settlement, Lake Rotopounamu, or Lake Taupō itself, which has some hot springs. However, this region lies considerably more than two days' riding from Wellington. Kaiwharawhara itself, a few miles outside Wellington, was by 1859 a largely European village. More likely, Krull is referring to a traditional occupation site known as Kaiwherowhero, in the Gladstone area of Wairarapa. That would have been about the right distance away, and consistent with much of his description of the location. Another possibility is a site near Lake Wairarapa to the south.

17. The famous chief Te Wherowhero lived a long way north in the Waikato and became the first Māori King in 1858; he died on June 25, 1860. Possibly, if the place Krull visited was Kaiwherowhero, he may have been confusing the place name with a chief whose name was publicly prominent at this time because of tensions between the government and the Māori King movement, which would eventually result in the invasion of the Waikato in 1863.

18. A Miss Hunt was listed among the passengers who sailed to Wellington on board the *Equator*.

19. Mrs Edwards offered board and lodgings at her residence on Willis Street, next to St Peter's Anglican Church which had opened in 1848 and had major renovations in 1857.

20. Krull may be referring to either The Royal Olympic, which

had started life in Manners Street as the Royal Victoria, New Zealand's first purpose-built theatre, or the Royal Lyceum on Willis Street, previously known as the Britannia Saloon.

March 18th, 1859

21. It is not clear where Krull lived in 1859. His business, Krull & Co., Merchants, was listed in an 1866 Wellington directory as based on Customhouse Quay.

22. Bishop Selwyn's 'High Church' leanings and evident sympathy for Māori causes did not endear him to many settlers.

23. Wellington had suffered two major earthquakes since European settlement began, the first in 1848 and the second in 1855. The 1855 quake, 8.2 on the Richter scale, is still the largest ever recorded in New Zealand. It caused a tsunami in the harbour and altered the shoreline considerably.

24. Possibly the case of Pickett v. Ngarara, heard in the Wellington Resident Magistrate's Court on March 16, 1859. Ngarara, having been found guilty of stealing a cap from Pickett, was found guilty and ordered to pay five times the value of the stolen article in restitution.

April 14th, 1859

25. Eight prisoners working as a chain gang escaped from Wellington gaol on the morning of April 4, 1859. However, no one was murdered. Three of the men were still on the run several weeks later, prompting concerns for public safety.

26. Australia

27. The only known islands are Mana and Kāpiti; both are quite large.

28. Probably Paekākāriki Hill, the summit of which is 250 metres, or 820 feet.

29. Krull is probably referring to the pursuit of supporters of Ngāti Toa chief Te Rangihaeata through the Waikanae district in 1846. Te Rangihaeata had strenuously opposed the New Zealand Company's move to claim ownership of the Hutt Valley and was deemed to be in arms against the government.

30. A colourful story, but lacking any foundation in fact.

31. A town in Mecklenburg, Germany.

32. In the 1830s Tamihana Te Rauparaha, son of Ngāti Toa chief Te Rauparaha, and his cousin Mātene Te Whiwhi had persuaded the Church Missionary Society to send a preacher to Waikanae. Reverend Octavius Hadfield arrived in November 1839 and began to conduct services, eventually being instrumental in the building of the Rangiātea Church at Ōtaki. As importantly, he had knowledge of wheat farming, and by 1850 Māori had several hundred acres at Waikanae and Ōtaki under cultivation.

33. Tamihana Te Rauparaha was Te Rauparaha's only surviving son and Mātene Te Whiwhi his nephew. Mātene converted to Christianity in 1841 and became a missionary. He and Tamihana undertook a long journey around the South Island making peace with Te Rauparaha's old enemies, Ngāi Tahu. In 1851 Tamihana travelled to England; he returned with a mission to establish a Māori monarchy along the lines of the British, seeing it as a way of bringing peace to the country. The two men travelled widely promoting the idea. Later, other

Māori took up the cause and in 1857 an ageing Waikato chief, Pōtatau Te Wherowhero, was selected as the first king.

34. A number of paintings and sketches of Te Rauparaha exist, but the whereabouts of this carefully described oil painting, possibly by Charles Barraud or William Beetham, is today unknown.

35. In fact the Waikato chief Pōtatau Te Wherowhero had been installed as king at Ngaruawahia the previous year. It is possible the meeting was held to ask local Māori to support him and the aims of the King movement.

36. Rangiātea Church, completed in 1851.

37. Probably Riwai Te Ahu, Hadfield's assistant, who was ordained in 1858.

38. St Mary's Church was built in 1858–59 and survives as New Zealand's oldest Catholic church still in use.

May 25th, 1859

39. Governor Gore Browne wrote to Donald McLean, the government's land purchase commissioner, on April 11, 1859, 'I propose to go to Wellington on the White Swan ... We give the Ball usually given on the Queens's birthday on the 25th April, and the Brig is to leave for Wellington after that as soon as she pleases. Under all the circumstances, I shall land quietly at Wellington, so do not be surprised if you do not see the flag up. Say nothing of this to others. We may as well go on to Wanganui as soon as we can...' Soon after this he visited Ōtaki with McLean to canvass land sales. The methods by which McLean arranged land sales were controversial: the English translation

of a letter from Tamihana Te Rauparaha to McLean dated June 17 refers to 'discussions following your departure' and 'arguments between Ngatihuia and Ngatiparo regarding the areas set aside at Te Horo for sale'. On March 30, 1860 a petition signed by 508 local Māori, unhappy with Gore Browne's actions in Taranaki, asked the Queen to recall him as governor.

40. The deed of purchase from members of Ngāti Toa for an area estimated at more than 30,000 acres and known as the Wainui block was finalised in June 1859, with £850 paid for the land. A down payment had been made in April 1858.

41. This was remarkably accurate. Modern mapping shows it is 66.4 million acres.

42. The first New Zealand parliament had sat in Auckland in 1854; by 1856 it held more power than the governor.

43. Two of these were the *New Zealand Spectator and Cook's Strait Guardian* and the *Wellington Independent*. The third was probably the *New Zealand Advertiser*, a pioneering giveaway newspaper.

44. Born in Taranaki, Honiana Te Puni-kokopu took part in the great overland migration of 1832, escaping Waikato invaders, and eventually settled at Pito-one. He did business with land purchasers on the New Zealand Company ship the *Tory*, signed the Treaty of Waitangi, and became a firm friend and ally of the settlers and Governor George Grey, who replaced Gore Browne in 1861.

45. The head was (and is) considered the most deeply tapu part of the body. In earlier times those who touched the head of a great rangatira could indeed expect to pay the ultimate price for their action.

46. This name appears to be spelled phonetically. The man's identity is not known.

47. Krull was probably referring to Whanganui, where a short conflict had broken out between two tribes disputing the ownership of valuable lands.

48. Government efforts after March 1859 to push through with the purchase of lands at Waitara in the Taranaki district, against the determined opposition of Wiremu Kingi Te Rangitake and other customary owners, were thought likely to result in fighting between Māori and Pākehā. When Kingi and other owners resisted the forcible survey of the lands in March 1860, they were attacked by British troops, sparking the first Taranaki War of 1860–61.

February 7th, 1862

49. August Weyergang had become a naturalised New Zealander in October 1856. His occupation was given as schoolmaster.

50. Johann Friederich August Kelling, also known as Fedor Kelling, had emigrated to New Zealand in 1844, along with his brother Carl Friederich Christian Kelling, settling in Nelson. The brothers were appointed agents for a successful scheme to attract German migrants to the region. Fedor Kelling later served on the Nelson Provincial Council, briefly as a member of parliament, and was later appointed as a German consul in New Zealand. He received the Order of the Crown of Prussia for his services.

51. Plattdeutsch, also known as Low German, is said to come from Old Saxon and was largely spoken in northern Germany and the east of The Netherlands. Today it is officially recognised as

a regional language by the governments of Germany and The Netherlands and efforts are being made to preserve it.

52. An entailed estate is one in which property inheritance is restricted by limiting it to the owner's lineal descendants.

53. Carl Friederich Christian (Charles) Kelling, Fedor's elder brother, had moved in 1850 to Sarau (Upper Moutere).

54. Probably the merchant Charles Petschler, who was naturalised in Auckland on April 21, 1855.

55. Fritz Reuter, born in Mecklenburg in 1810, was a well-known poet and author who wrote in Low German. His first collection of poems was published in 1853 and a second in 1858. A two-metre high bronze statue of him stands in the town of Neubrandenburg, where he did much of his writing.

56. The flag of Rostock, a northern German city on the Baltic Sea.

57. Shipping logs of the time record the ship as the 429-ton *Margaretha Roesner* under Captain Christian Eggers.

ILLUSTRATIONS

All illustrations are from the collections of Alexander Turnbull Library, Wellington, New Zealand, unless otherwise stated.

opposite page 1: Wellington Harbour with bush and house roofs in the foreground, three steam and sailing ships, Matiu/Somes Island and the eastern hills behind, 1880s. Probably a view from above Stowe Hill, Thorndon, where the artist lived.
WATERCOLOUR BY JANE STOWE (1838–1931), A-178-015

page 7: Johann Friederich August (Fedor) Kelling (1820–1909), Nelson-based emigration agent, farmer and community leader, circa 1895. Kelling was the first German elected to the New Zealand parliament, served from 1859–1860, and later became a German Consul.
PHOTOGRAPHER UNKNOWN, C.M. HEINE COLLECTION, PACOLL-4187-1-01

page 10: The *Equator*, the ship on which Friedrich Krull arrived in New Zealand in January 1859; drawing dated December 12, 1858.
PENCIL AND CHINESE WHITE DRAWING BY WILLIAM GILBERT REES (1827–1898), E-199-Q-038

page 16: Mount Egmont/Taranaki and Sugar Loaf/Ngā Motu Islands, Taranaki, 1849.
WATERCOLOUR AND CHINESE WHITE DRAWING WITH SCRAPING OUT BY CHARLES HEAPHY (1820–1881), A-145-011

page 18: Wellington Harbour and sailing craft, circa 1850s.
WATERCOLOUR BY CHARLES EMILIUS GOLD (1809–1871), A-288-004

page 21: Te Aro flat, Wellington, circa 1860s, showing Rhodes and Company wharf and Rhodes residence on the left, Kebbells Mill (building with arched roof, later site of Grand Opera House) and Market Hall (castle-like building), built 1865.
PHOTOGRAPHER UNKNOWN, F-21186-1/2

page 22: Typical Thorndon cottage on Molesworth Street, 1860s.
PHOTOGRAPHER UNKNOWN, F-21155-1/2

page 26: Twenty-eight-year-old German geologist Ferdinand von Hochstetter, 1859.
LITHOGRAPH BY ADOLF DAUTHAGE (1825–1883), PUBL-0135-front

page 29: View from the Percy family property (later Percy Scenic Reserve) in Maungaraki, looking south down the Hutt Valley towards Petone, Matiu/Somes Island and Wellington Harbour, late 1860s. In the left foreground is Percy's Flour Mill.
PHOTOGRAPH BY JAMES BRAGGE (1833–1908), JAMES BRAGGE COLLECTION, F-13373-1/1

page 30: View past dense bush, including a large tree covered with epiphytes, looking towards still water. Possibly the Hutt Forest and part of the Hutt River, circa 1850.
WATERCOLOUR BY CHARLES EMILIUS GOLD (1809–1871), A-288-029

page 31: Kākāriki from Ship Cove and Te Awaiti, Marlborough Sounds, August 1839.
WATERCOLOUR BY CHARLES HEAPHY (1820–1881), C-025-007

page 33: Two Māori men and a seated woman with tree fern at sunset, possibly Hutt Valley, circa 1848.
WATERCOLOUR AND GOUACHE ON PAPER BY LIEUTENANT FREDERICK JOHN WHITE (1837–1848), A-292-075

page 35: Māori family at a cutting on the Rimutaka hill road from

Hutt Valley to Wairarapa, September 1854.
WATERCOLOUR AND INK DRAWING BY JOHN PEARSE (1808–1882),
E-455-F-073-1

page 36: Māori family outside a wharepuni, a small communal
sleeping house, at Mangakuta near Masterton, 1870s. The
wharepuni has on the gables a painted record of the legend of
Maui fishing up the North Island and so is sometimes referred to
as the Maui house. The family members are antecedents of the
Reiri family.
PHOTOGRAPHER UNKNOWN, J.D. ROBINS COLLECTION, PACOLL-0260-1

page 39: Māori horse race with many participants and spectators
on the Ruamahanga Plain, Wairarapa, 1852.
ARTIST UNKNOWN. WOOD ENGRAVING FROM *ILLUSTRATED LONDON NEWS*,
VOL. 23, NO. 656. DEC. 10, 1853, P. 497, PUBL-0033-1853-0479

page 40: Cattle on the banks of the Ruamahanga River in south
Wairarapa, circa 1863.
WATERCOLOUR AND CHINESE WHITE PAINTING BY CHARLES DECIMUS
BARRAUD (1822–1897), C-007-016

page 42: Three Māori, two men and one woman, riding on
horseback, 1856. The woman wears a top hat and the men peaked
caps. The woman rides side-saddle. The artist has written: 'A group
I once saw in Maori Land, New Plymouth'.
PENCIL AND WASH DRAWING BY WILLIAM STRUTT (1825–1915), E-453-F-005

page 45: E Rangi and E Tohi of Port Nicholson Pa with Kiko, an old
woman of Tiakiwai kāinga, 1844.
WATERCOLOUR BY GEORGE FRENCH ANGAS (1822–1866), PUBL-0014-31.
ORIGINAL WORK HELD IN FLETCHER TRUST COLLECTION.

page 47: Looking up Willis Street from Clay Point at the junction
of Willis Street and Lambton Quay, with Warmoll's Outfitting

Establishment on the corner on the right and the Commercial Hotel (site of the later Grand Hotel in Willis Street) in the centre.
PHOTOGRAPHER UNKNOWN, F-000694-1/1

page 50: Pioneer cottages, Cuba Street, Wellington, 1864. The cottage on the left with the sign was the house and factory of Edward Dixon, a cordial and ginger beer manufacturer.
PHOTOGRAPHER UNKNOWN, F-060601-1/2

page 53: George Augustus Selwyn (1809–1878), Anglican Bishop of New Zealand, circa 1869.
PHOTOGRAPH BY FRED WHITLOCK, PA2-1920

page 55: Banks of the Hutt River near Mr Molesworth's farm. A Māori warrior with red cloak and club stands on the riverbank at right and two waka approach along the river. A large cabbage tree overhangs the river. Mr Molesworth's house and outbuildings are on the far bank.
DRAWING BY SAMUEL CHARLES BREES (1810–1865); ENGRAVING BY HENRY MELVILLE, LONDON, 1847, PUBL-0020-14-2

page 58: View from the hill above Pukerua Bay, looking north up the coast and across the Paekākāriki cliffs. Kāpiti Island is visible, as is the cone of Mount Taranaki on the horizon, far left. In the foreground a Māori family is crossing the Taua-Tapu track, a Ngāti Toa trail from Plimmerton to Paekākāriki that continued along the coast. A few houses can be seen on the Pukerua beach.
DRAWING BY SAMUEL CHARLES BREES (1810–1865); ENGRAVING BY HENRY MELVILLE, LONDON, 1849, E-070-019

page 60: Kāpiti and Mana Islands, with Cook Strait beyond, circa 1855.
WATERCOLOUR AND INK DRAWING BY JOHN PEARSE (1808–1882), E-455-F-081-3

page 63: Paikakariki (Paekākāriki) hill road, looking out to Kāpiti Island, November 22, 1877.
PENCIL AND WATERCOLOUR DRAWING BY CHARLES DECIMUS BARRAUD (1822–1897), A-084-017-1

page 64: A group of Māori and Pākehā near a beach, probably Paekākāriki, looking towards Pukerua, circa 1845.
WATERCOLOUR BY SAMUEL CHARLES BREES (1810–1865), B-031-004

page 66: Trochus imperialis: 'Found only at New Zealand, and here it is rare; the shell is very beautiful, the whorls rising in a depressed cone' (Samuel Griswold Goodrich, 1859).
ARTIST UNKNOWN. ENGRAVING FROM S.G. GOODRICH, *ILLUSTRATED NATURAL HISTORY OF THE ANIMAL KINGDOM*, VOL. 2, DERBY & JACKSON, NEW YORK, 1859

page 67: Nikau palms in the Wellington region, circa 1848–1860.
WATERCOLOUR BY CHARLES EMILIUS GOLD (1809–1871), A-288-006

page 69: Mātene, or Martin, Te Whiwhi, Ngāti Toa and Ngāti Raukawa leader, missionary, and a founder of the Māori King movement, circa 1870. His mother was Ngāti Toa chieftainess Te Rangi Topeora and his father Te Rangikapiki of Ngāti Raukawa. He was born and raised at Kawhia and participated in the migration Te Heke Tahu-tahu-ahi about 1821. He lived at Ōtaki, adopted Christianity, and with his cousin Tamihana Te Rauparaha went to fetch Octavius Hadfield as a missionary for his people. When baptised by Hadfield in 1843 he took the names Henare Mātene. He died in 1881.
PHOTOGRAPHER UNKNOWN, G. CLARKE COLLECTION, F-57403-1/2

page 71: Tamihana, or Thompson, Te Rauparaha, son of Ngāti Toa chief Te Rauparaha and his fifth wife Te Akau of Tuhourangi, dressed in a formal English suit and leaning against a half-pillar or desk, a book, probably a bible, under his left hand, 1852. Tamihana Te Rauparaha was born in Pukearuhe in Taranaki during the Ngāti

Toa migration south and took the name Tamihana when baptised by Octavius Hadfield in 1841. He travelled to England in 1850 and returned determined there should be a Māori monarchy, which was established in 1858. Two years later he broke with the movement when fighting broke out in Taranaki; he opposed the raising of the king's flag in Ōtaki.

WATERCOLOUR BY GEORGE FRENCH ANGAS (1822–1886), C-114-001

page 72: Tamihana Te Rauparaha's house at Ōtaki. Built in a combined Māori and European style, it had carved figures supporting the trellis around the front verandah, weatherboards and a shingled roof. The inside was also partially carved, with tukutuku panels on the walls. A young wisteria was trained to climb the roof pole. Other dwellings, possibly in the same style, can be seen in the background. The work is captioned: 'Thompson's Warree [sic], Otaki, New Zealand, 1849'.

WATERCOLOUR BY CHARLES EMILIUS GOLD (1809-1871), B-103-028

page 74: Inside Rangiātea Church, Ōtaki, with Māori listening to a sermon by Octavius Hadfield, circa 1850s or early 1860s.

LITHOGRAPH BY CHARLES DECIMUS BARRAUD (1822–1897); HAND-COLOURED PRINTED CALICO BY UNKNOWN ARTIST, D-010-002

page 76: Interior of Rangiātea Church, Ōtaki, showing the carved wooden altar rails, altar and tukutuku panels. There are two gas lamps on the wall above the altar, and an inscription on the wall, 'Ko Ahau Te Huarahi, Te Pono, Me Te Ora' ('I am the way, the truth and the life'), is partly revealed. Rangiātea was the oldest Māori Anglican church in New Zealand until destroyed by fire in 1995.

PHOTOGRAPH BY ALBERT PERCY GODBER (1875–1949), A.P. GODBER COLLECTION, G-0103-1/2-APG

page 80: Buildings on the corner of Cuba and Ghuznee Streets in Wellington, including premises of Kirkcaldie & Stains, General Drapers, circa 1860s.

PHOTOGRAPHER UNKNOWN, V. BONTHORNE COLLECTION, F-31688-1/2

page 85: Thomas Robert Gore Browne, governor of New Zealand 1855–1861, with his wife, daughter, son and private secretary, circa 1859.
PHOTOGRAPH BY JOHN NICOL CROMBIE (1827–1878), URQUHART ALBUM, PA1-Q-250-06

page 86: Front and side view of Provincial Council Assembly building, Wellington. Probably taken soon after its completion in 1858.
PHOTOGRAPH BY GEORGE HENRY SWAN (1833–1913), G.H. SWAN COLLECTION, F-3739-1/2

page 88: Hot springs at Tokaanu near Lake Taupō, October 26, 1844.
WATERCOLOUR BY GEORGE FRENCH ANGAS (1822–1886), A-020-038

page 89: Close-up view of a geyser with twin spout and silica formations, Wairakei, 1886.
OIL PAINTING BY CHARLES BLOMFIELD (1848–1926), G-511

page 90: Interior of a whare, probably at Pito-one (Petone), with Honiana Te Puni-kokopu sitting on the ground beside a fire, a small dog asleep beside him, 1860. A taiaha leans on the wall at the left, and on the far wall hang a kete and musket. Te Puni wears a dogskin cloak and an earring. Through the open doorway can be seen a canoe drawn up on the shore of Wellington Harbour and a group of three figures (two kneeling, apparently blowing on a fire below a cauldron) close to a gap in a fence of wooden spiked poles. A hill, probably of the western hills near Petone, is visible in the background.
WATERCOLOUR BY CHARLES DECIMUS BARRAUD (1822–1897), B-005-015

page 96: Port Nelson, Port Hills, Haven Road and wharves, across mudflats from Wakapuaka, circa 1860.
PHOTOGRAPHER UNKNOWN, NELSON PROVINCIAL MUSEUM, COPY COLLECTION, C294

page 99: The Lutheran parsonage at Upper Moutere, with Reverend Johann Wilhelm Christoph Heine (1814–1900) seated in the garden, 1880s.
PHOTOGRAPHER UNKNOWN, MISS C.W. HEINE COLLECTION, G-032576-1/2

page 100: Fiftieth wedding anniversary of the Reverend and Mrs Johann Wilhelm Christoph Heine (née Anna Bensemann), September 5, 1899, probably at Upper Moutere. Child in foreground: John Erle Schroder. Front row: Gertrude Heine, Mrs J. Thiel (née Heine), Joseph Heine. Second row from front (seated): Reverend J. Thiel, Reverend J.W.C. Heine and Mrs Heine, Dietrich Wilkens, Fedor Kelling (also known as Johann Friederich Augustus Kelling), Mrs F. Schroder. Third row from front (standing): Mrs George Bensemann, Mrs H. Bensemann, Frederick Bensemann, Mrs D. Max, Mrs D. Wilkens, Henry B., David Max, F. Schroder. Back row: J.H.C. Drogemuller, George Bensemann, Fedor Kelling Jr, Heinrich Darel (standing above), John Muller, unidentified, unidentified.
PHOTOGRAPHER UNKNOWN, C.M. HEINE COLLECTION, G-032577-1/2

page 104: Friedrich Krull in the uniform of Consul for the German Empire to New Zealand, date unknown. He was appointed Consul in 1871 at the age of thirty-six.
PHOTOGRAPHER UNKNOWN, COLLECTION OF WHANGANUI REGIONAL MUSEUM

page 106: Wellington from the Post Office tower, circa 1880s. The view looks over Lambton Quay and The Terrace towards Kelburn. Wellington Athenaeum and Mechanics Institute (with clock tower), Bank of New South Wales, South British Insurance, fire bell tower, Roman Catholic School in Boulcott Street, and Friedrich Krull's garden and gazebo are all visible.
PHOTOGRAPH BY BURTON BROTHERS, BURTON BROTHERS COLLECTION, F-18794-1/2

page 107: Friedrich Krull with his wife and family on the veranda of their home in Whanganui, early 1900s. The Krull family moved to the town in 1884.
PHOTOGRAPHER UNKNOWN, COLLECTION OF WHANGANUI REGIONAL MUSEUM

INDEX

Page references in *italics* refer to illustrations.